GETTING TO KNOW THE WORLD'S GREATEST ARTISTS

RAPHAEL

WRITTEN AND ILLUSTRATED BY MIKE VENEZIA

CHILDREN'S PRESS®
A DIVISION OF GROLIER PUBLISHING
NEW YORK   LONDON   HONG KONG   SYDNEY
DANBURY, CONNECTICUT

Cover: *The Sistine Madonna*, by Raphael (Raffaello Sanzio of Urbino)(1483-1520). c. 1513. Oil on canvas, 269.5 x 201 cm. Gemaeldegalerie, Staatliche Kunstsammlungen, Dresden, Germany. © Bridgeman Art Library International Ltd., London/New York (BAL 76904).

Colorist for illustrations: Liz Venezia

Library of Congress Cataloging-in-Publication Data

Venezia, Mike.
   Raphael / written and illustrated by Mike Venezia.
     p. cm. — (Getting to know the world's greatest artists)
   ISBN 0-516-22028-4 (lib. bdg.)   0-516-27285-3 (pbk.)
   1. Raphael, 1483-1520—Juvenile literature. 2.
Painters—Italy—Biography—Juvenile literature. [1. Raphael, 1483-1520.
2. Artists. 3. Painting, Italian. 4. Painting, Renaissance—Italy.] I. Title
   ND623.R2 V37 2001
   759.5—dc21
                                                  00-040434

Visit Children's Press on the Internet at:
http://publishing.grolier.com

GROLIER
PUBLISHING

Self-portrait, by Raphael. 1506. Oil on poplar, 113 x 88.5 cm. Galleria degli Uffizi, Florence, Italy. © Scala/Art Resource, NY.

Raphael Sanzio was born in the beautiful hill town of Urbino, Italy, in 1483. Raphael, along with Leonardo da Vinci and Michelangelo, became one of the greatest and best-loved artists during a very important time in European history known as the High Renaissance.

The Annunciation, by Raphael. 1502. 27 x 50 cm.
Pinacoteca, Vatican Museums, Vatican State.
© Scala/Art Resource, NY

Throughout his life, Raphael painted pictures of religious events, people, and exciting legends.

Portrait of a Woman with a Unicorn, by Raphael.
c. 1505. 65 x 51 cm. Galleria Borghese, Rome, Italy.
© Scala/Art Resource, NY.

Saint George and the Dragon, by Raphael. c. 1506. Oil on panel, 28 x 22 cm. Andrew W. Mellon Collection.
© National Gallery of Art, Washington, DC.

The Small Cowper Madonna, by Raphael. c. 1505. Oil on panel, 59 x 44 cm. Widener Collection. © National Gallery of Art, Washington, DC.

Raphael's most popular works were his paintings of the Madonna and Child. People loved the way Raphael showed the love between the baby Jesus and his mother Mary. Raphael's crystal-clear lighting gave a special dimension and feeling to his figures that had never been seen before. Raphael's people seem real. You can almost feel the weight of Raphael's beautiful, plump babies.

Tempi Madonna, by Raphael. c. 1508. Oil on panel, 75 x 51 cm. Alte Pinakothek, Munich, Germany.
© Scala/Art Resource, NY.

Photograph of Urbino, Italy. © Scala/Art Resource, NY.

The Renaissance was an important period in history because it was the first time in hundreds of years that kings, dukes, and religious leaders began caring about people's rights. They started to realize the importance of education, and began filling their cities with beautiful works of art.

Baptism of Christ, by Piero della Francesca (c.1419-1492). 1450s. Egg tempera on poplar panel, 167 x 116 cm. National Gallery, London, UK. © Bridgeman Art Library International Ltd., London/New York (PHD 372).

The duke who ran Urbino was particularly interested in making it a showplace. He hired the best artists in Europe, including Piero della Francesca and Paolo Uccello, to decorate the walls of buildings and churches. He welcomed writers, poets, architects, and scientists, too.

The Battle of San Romano, by Paolo Uccello. c. 1456. Distemper on wood panel, 182 x 323 cm. National Gallery, London, UK. © Erich Lessing/ Art Resource, NY.

While Raphael was growing up in Urbino, he was able to see great works of art all over the place. He also got to meet many of the artists who visited his father's studio and workshop.

Raphael's father was a well-known artist in Urbino. Although no one is sure, it seems likely that he taught his son about art when Raphael was very young.

The Assumption of the Virgin, by Pietro Perugino. 1506. 333 x 218 cm. Accademia, Florence, Italy. © Scala/Art Resource, NY.

When Raphael was fourteen or fifteen years old, he left Urbino and traveled to the nearby town of Perugia. He went there to learn from Pietro Perugino, one of the greatest artists in Italy. In Perugino's workshop, Raphael studied hard to learn everything he could.

Raphael was such a good student that Perugino trusted him to paint certain sections of his own works. Some experts think Raphael painted St. Benedict and St. Michael in Perugino's altarpiece. They are the two figures on the bottom right side of the painting shown on page 12. Soon Raphael's and Perugino's paintings started to look very much alike.

The Marriage of the Virgin, by Pietro Perugino. c. 1503. Panel, 236 x 186 cm. Musée des Beaux-Arts, Caen, France. © Erich Lessing/Art Resource, NY.

One of Raphael's special talents was that he was able to learn in a very short time what had taken his teachers years to perfect. He then put the things he learned together in a way that was all his own.

For example, Raphael's *Marriage of the Virgin* is similar in many ways to Perugino's *Marriage of the Virgin*.

Raphael found a way to give his painting a greater feeling of space, though. He also gave his people more movement, and facial expressions that were more realistic.

The Marriage of the Virgin, by Raphael. 1504. 170 x 117 cm. Pinacoteca di Brera, Milan, Italy. © Scala/Art Resource, NY.

When Raphael was nineteen or twenty
years old, he traveled to Florence, Italy, to
study the great artists of the past, as well
as to learn from those who lived and worked
there at that time. Raphael was lucky
to see the work of Leonardo da Vinci and
Michelangelo. Both of these artists were
working in Florence when Raphael arrived.

Leonardo and Michelangelo were painting scenes on opposite walls of a large palace room. In a way, they were competing with each other. The people of Florence loved the idea that two of the most famous artists in the world were trying to outdo each other.

Raphael learned new things about composition from Leonardo da Vinci. After noticing how Leonardo sometimes arranged his figures into a kind of pyramid shape, Raphael tried the same thing. From Michelangelo, Raphael learned how to show natural movement of the human body.

Virgin and Child with St. Anne, by Leonardo da Vinci (1452-1519). c. 1510. Tempera and oil on wood, 168 x 130 cm. Louvre, Paris, France. © Bridgeman Art Library International Ltd., London/New York (BEN 505).

Libyan Sibyl, by Michelangelo. c. 1510. Fresco, 395 x 380 cm. Sistine Chapel, Vatican Palace, Vatican State. © Scala/Art Resource, NY.

Raphael's artwork improved more and more every day. Soon people all over Florence, as well as those in other nearby cities, were asking him to make paintings.

After spending four years in Florence, Raphael had become just about the most popular artist around. In 1508, the news of Raphael's remarkable art reached the attention of the wealthiest and most powerful leader in Italy, Pope Julius II.

Pope Julius was not only head of the Catholic Church in Rome, Italy, but an important military general. His armies protected the church's territories. Most importantly for Raphael, Pope Julius wanted to make Rome the most beautiful city in the world. The Pope invited Raphael to Rome to join Michelangelo and many other famous artists.

Portrait of Pope Julius II, by Raphael. c. 1506. Oil on wood, 107 x 80 cm. Galleria degli Uffizi, Florence, Italy. © Scala/Art Resource, NY.

Raphael's first job when he arrived in Rome was to decorate the walls of a large room in the Vatican, the Pope's palace. Even though he had never created anything that big before, Raphael jumped right in, designing and painting pictures that amazed everyone.

Raphael used all of his talents to create beautiful paintings that gave a feeling of real space. When you stand in front of one of these paintings, it feels almost as if the picture has come away from the wall and surrounded you!

The Disputa, by Raphael. c. 1509. Fresco, base 770 cm. Stanza della Segnatura, Vatican Palace, Vatican State. © Erich Lessing/Art Resource, NY.

The School of Athens, by Raphael. c. 1510. Fresco, base 770 cm.
Stanza della Segnatura, Vatican Palace, Vatican State. © Scala/Art Resource, NY.

On one wall of the palace room, Raphael painted a scene of the smartest teachers, poets, scientists, and mathematicians of ancient Greece. Since he didn't know what those ancient people looked like, Raphael used as models people he respected from his own time. The philosopher Plato, the

Detail from *The School of Athens* showing Plato
(a portrait of Leonardo da Vinci) talking with Aristotle.
© Erich Lessing/Art Resource, NY

Detail from *The School of Athens* showing what is
thought to be a portrait of Raphael. © Erich
Lessing/Art Resource, NY.

Detail from *The School of Athens* showing Heraclitus
(a portrait of Michelangelo). © Scala/Art Resource,
NY.

bearded man on the left at the top of the stairs, is modeled after Leonardo da Vinci. Raphael used himself as a model, too. He's way over on the right, wearing a black hat. The man writing at a desk is Michelangelo.

The Prophet Isaiah, by Michelangelo. c. 1510. Fresco, 365 x 380 cm. ceiling Sistine Chapel, Vatican Palace, Vatican State. © Scala/Art Resource, NY. Scala/Art Resource, NY.

Although Raphael greatly admired Michelangelo, Michelangelo had some problems with Raphael. He thought Raphael used too many of his ideas and

Isaiah, by Raphael. c.1511. Fresco, 250 x 155 cm. Church of Sant'Agostino, Rome, Italy. © Scala/Art Resource, NY.

discoveries in his own paintings. Michelangelo may also have been a little jealous of Raphael. It seemed like everyone was paying more attention to Raphael than Michelangelo, especially Pope Julius.

Raphael was Pope Julius' favorite artist. The Pope made sure Raphael was kept busy with all kinds of interesting jobs. Aside from decorating the palace rooms, Raphael became the head architect of the new St. Peter's Church. The Pope even put Raphael in charge of preserving important ancient Roman ruins that had just been discovered at that time.

Orpheus, Eurydice, and Hermes. Marble. Louvre, Paris, France. © Bridgeman Art Library International Ltd., London/New York (PWI 110877).

When Pope Julius died in 1518, a new Pope took over. Raphael got along with Pope Leo X, too. One of Raphael's greatest portraits is one he painted of the new Pope.

The Sistine Madonna, by Raphael (Raffaello Sanzio of Urbino)(1483-1520). c. 1513. Oil on canvas, 269.5 x 201 cm. Gemaeldegalerie, Staatliche Kunstsammlungen, Dresden, Germany. © Bridgeman Art Library International Ltd., London/New York (BAL 76904).

In 1512, Raphael painted what has become known as the *The Sistine Madonna*. It may be his best-loved picture. Raphael showed Mary and the baby Jesus standing in heavenly, crystal-clear light.

Raphael's colors balance his composition perfectly. One special touch that everyone loved is the two bored and mischievous cherubs at the bottom. If you look carefully, you can see little angel faces in the clouds near the top. *The Sistine Madonna* is so popular today that it is used on holiday greeting cards, posters, and calenders.

Madonna della Sedia, by Raphael. 1514. 71 cm. Galleria Palatina, Palazzo Pitti, Florence, Italy. © Scala/Art Resource, NY.

Raphael Sanzio died in 1520 on exactly the same day he was born. Raphael took the things he learned from the greatest artists of the day and formed them into his own special art. Raphael's peaceful, beautiful paintings made him one of the world's favorite artists during a remarkable time in the history of art.

Works of art in this book can be seen at the following places:

Accademia, Florence, Italy
Alte Pinakothek, Munich, Germany
Borghese Gallery, Rome, Italy
Church of Sant'Agostino, Rome, Italy
Gemaeldegalerie, Staatliche Kunstsammlungen, Dresden, Germany
Louvre, Paris, France
Musée des Beaux-Arts, Caen, France
National Gallery, London, Great Britain
National Gallery, Washington, D. C.
Palazzo Pitti, Florence, Italy
Pinacoteca de Brera, Milan, Italy
Pinacoteca, Vatican Museums, Vatican State
Sistine Chapel, Vatican Palace, Vatican State
Stanza della Segnatura, Vatican Palace, Vatican State
Uffizi Gallery, Florence, Italy